Tad's Tree

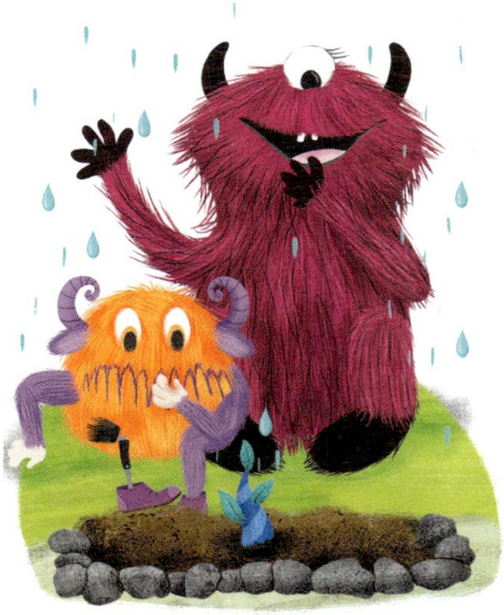

Written by Catherine Baker

Illustrated by Mel Armstrong

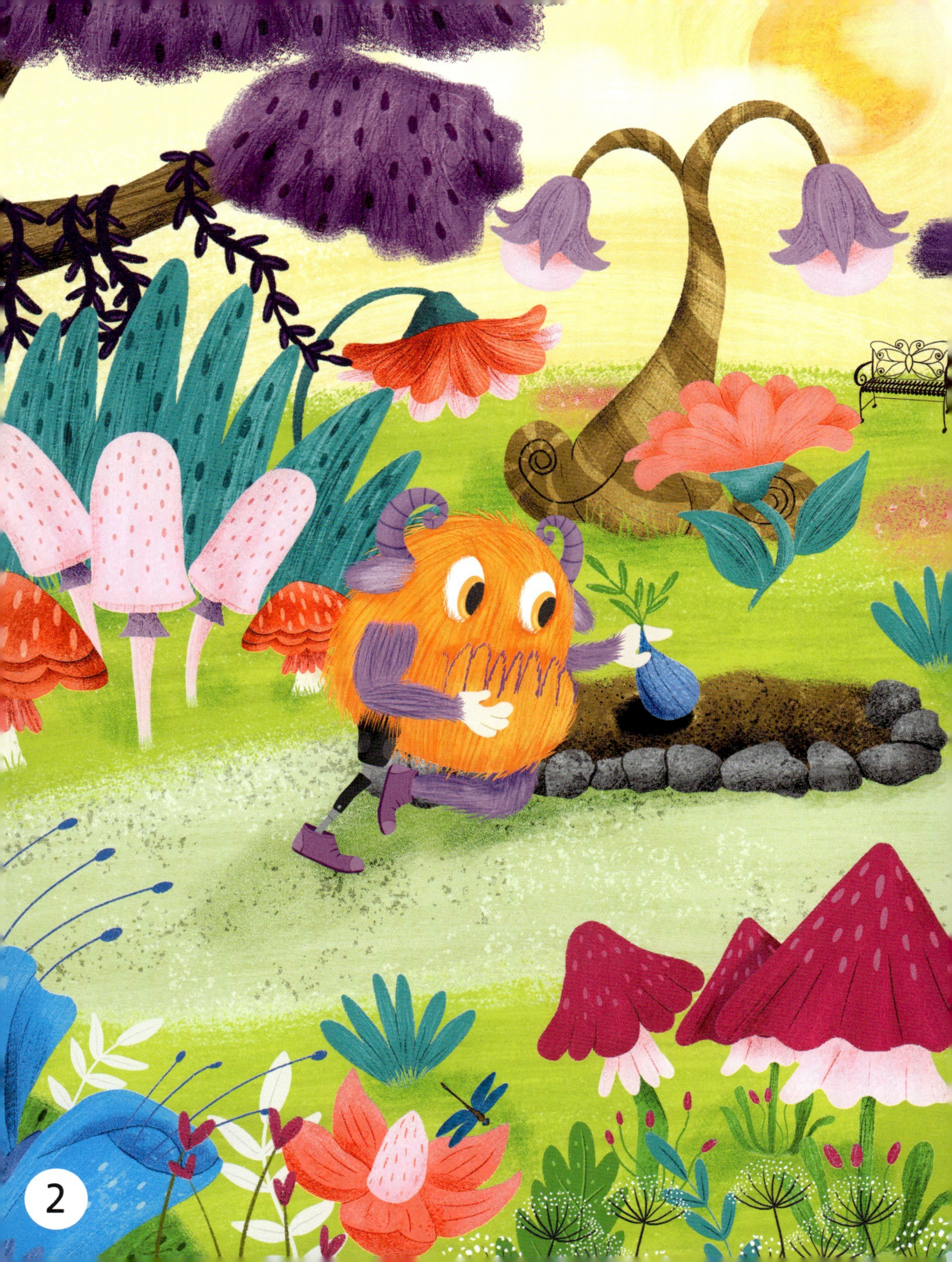

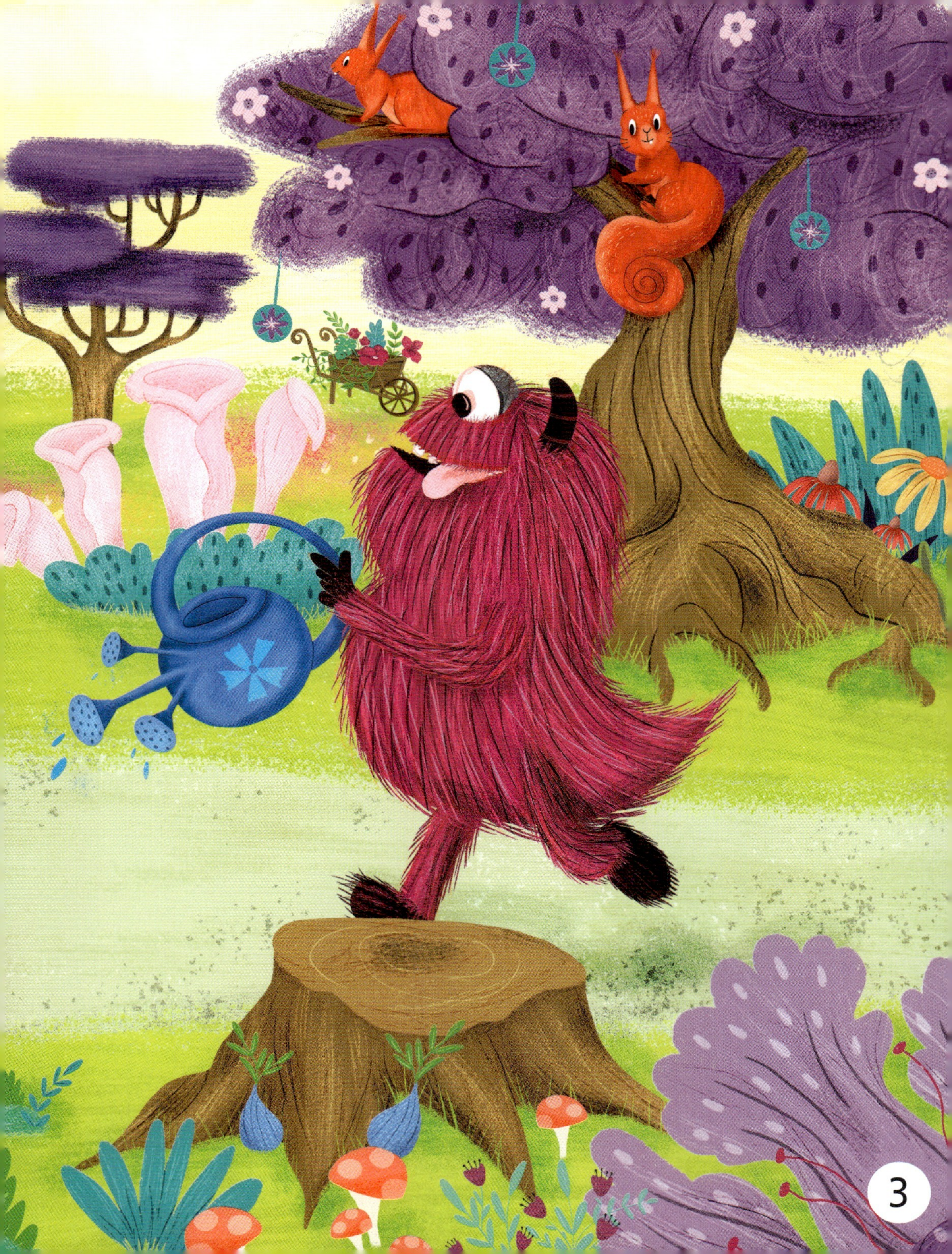

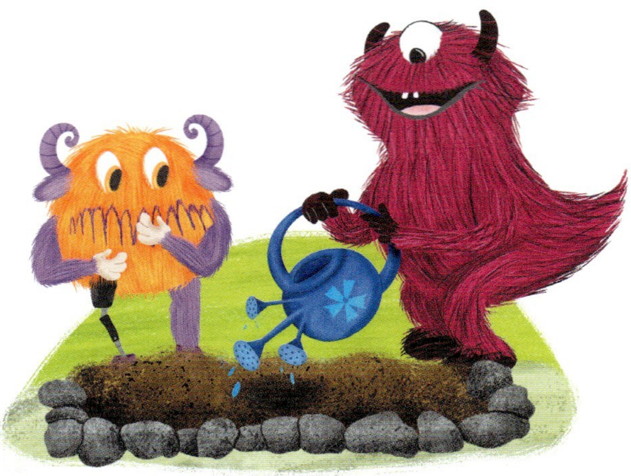

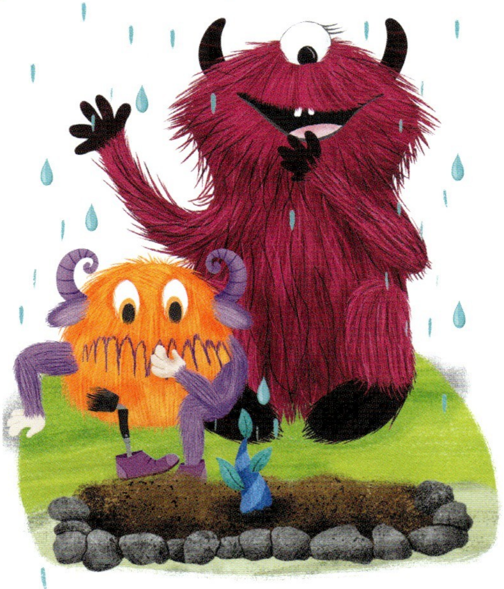

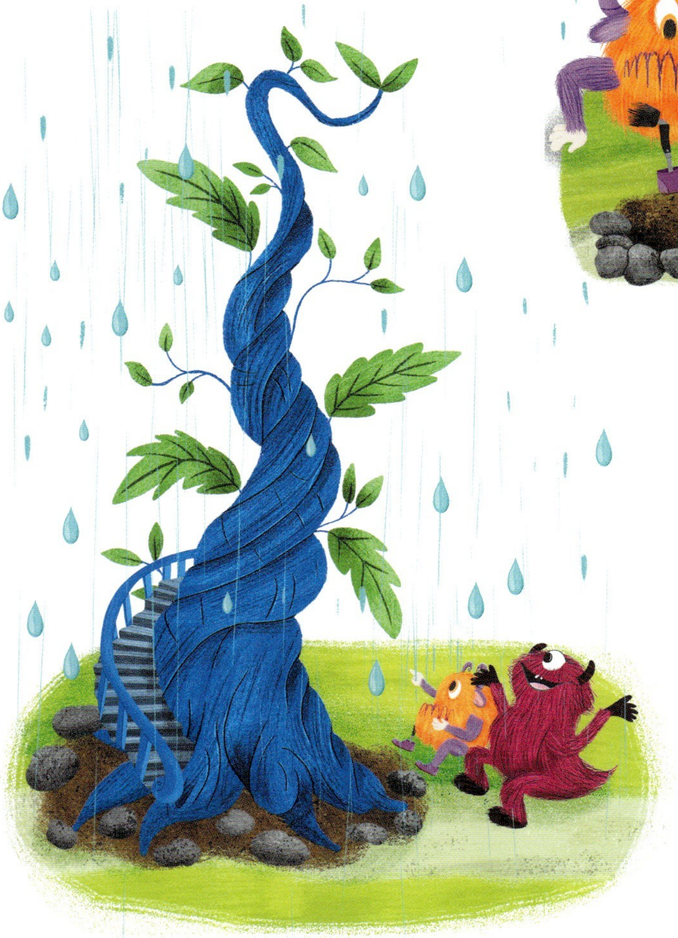

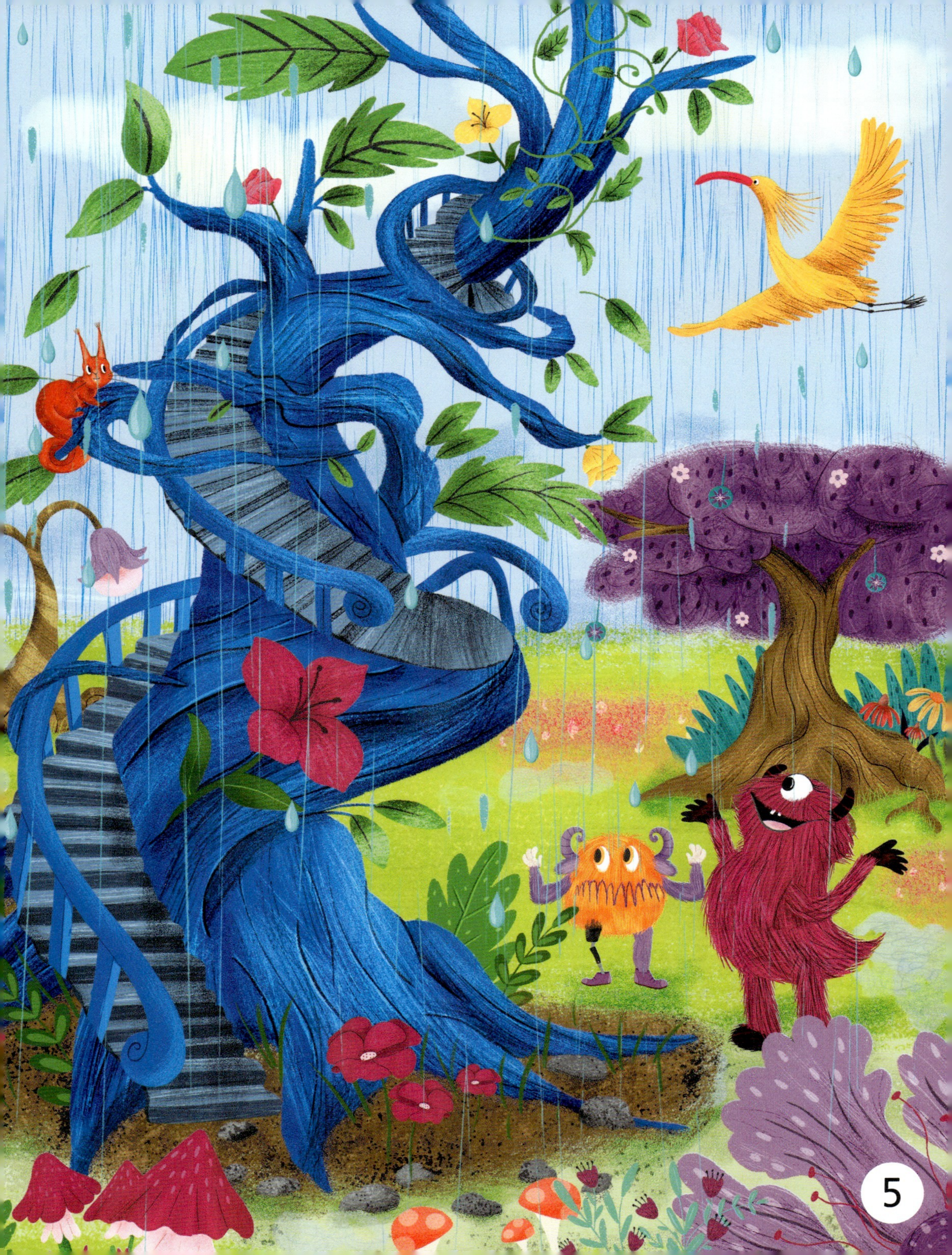

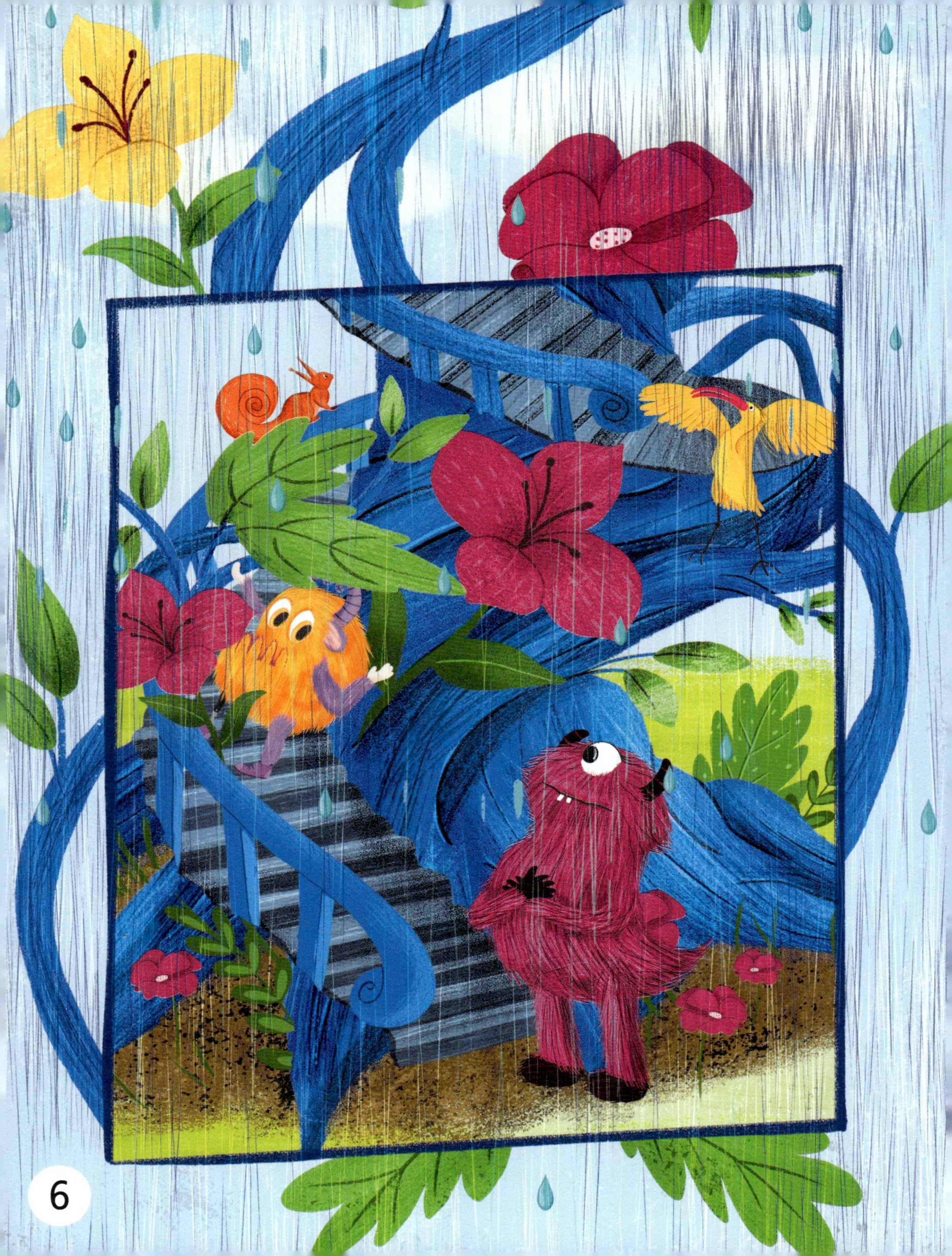

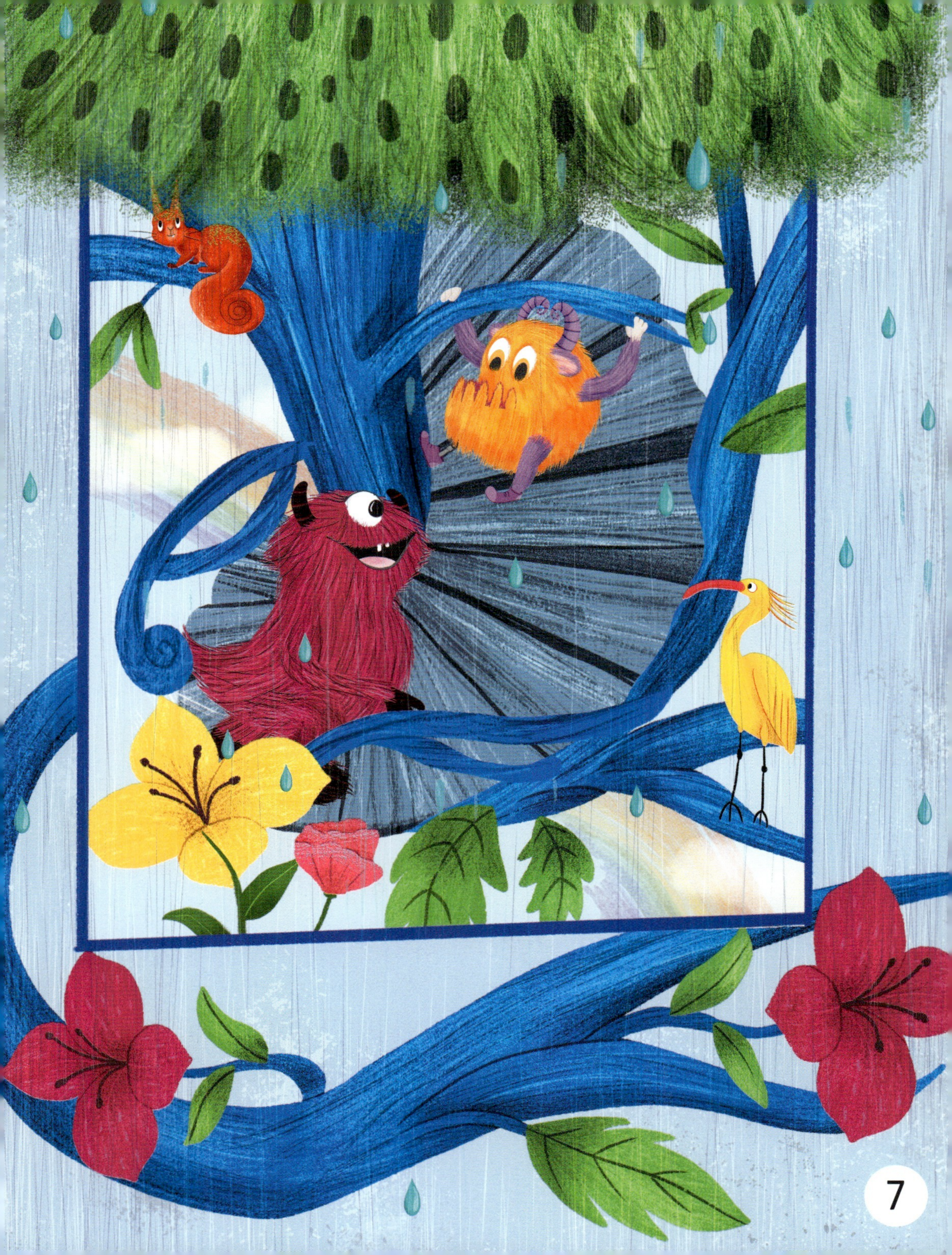

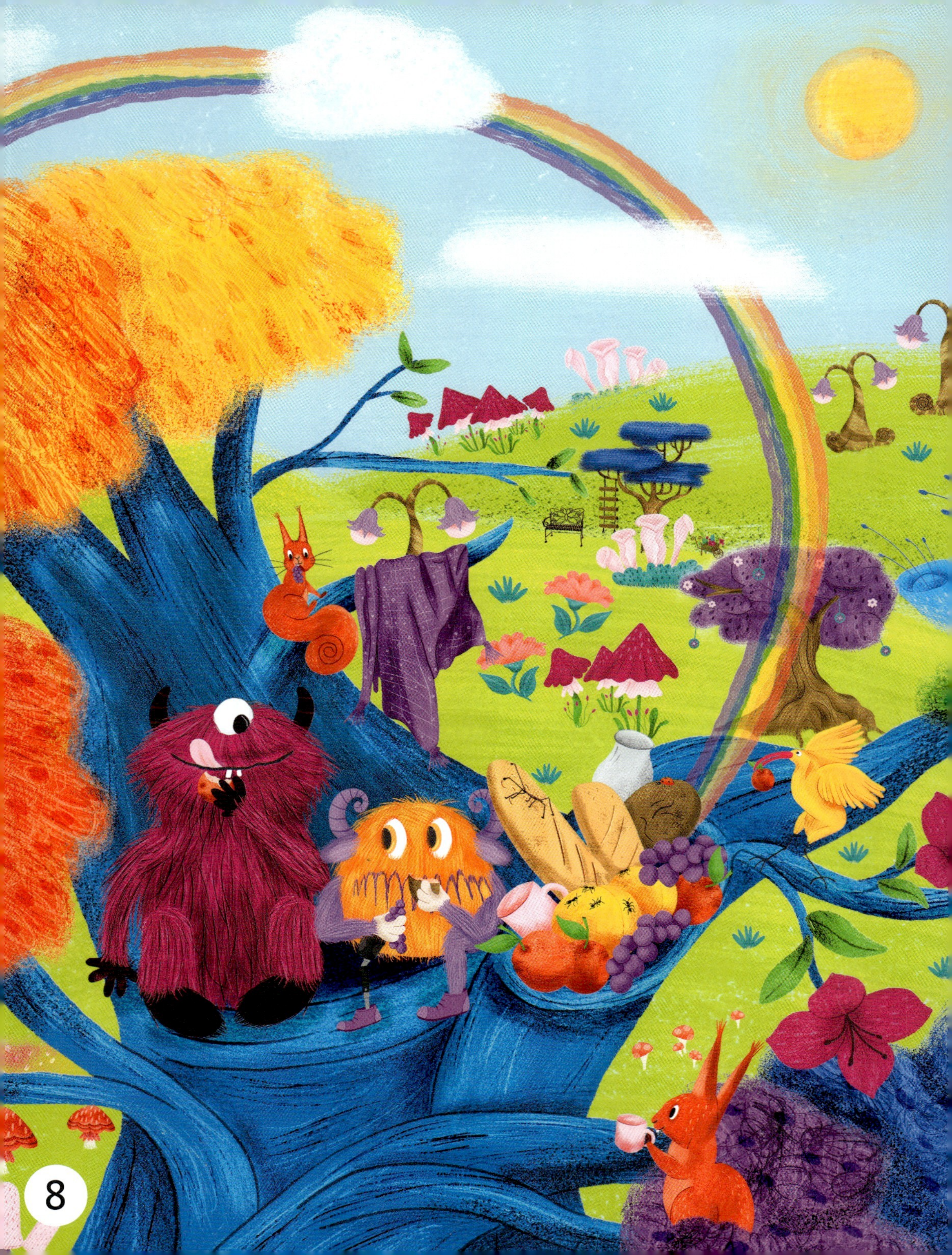